To:

_____

From:

_____

I
WISH
YOU
ENOUGH

EMBRACING LIFE'S *Most Valuable* MOMENTS

ONE WISH AT A TIME

BOB PERKS

THOMAS NELSON
Since 1798

NASHVILLE   DALLAS   MEXICO CITY   RIO DE JANEIRO   BEIJING

Published in Nashville, Tennessee, by Thomas Nelson®. Thomas Nelson is a registered trademark of Thomas Nelson, Inc.

Unless otherwise noted, Scripture quotations are taken from the NEW KING JAMES VERSION. © 1982 by Thomas Nelson, Inc. Used by permission. All rights reserved. HOLY BIBLE, NEW INTERNATIONAL VERSION® (NIV). Copyright © 1973, 1978, 1984 International Bible Society. Used by Permission of Zondervan. All right reserved.

Thomas Nelson, Inc., titles may be purchased in bulk for educational, business, fund-raising, or sales promotional use. For information, please e-mail SpecialMarkets@ThomasNelson.com.

Project Manager: Lisa Stilwell
Cover and interior design by Susan Browne Design, Nashville, TN

ISBN-13: 978-1-4041-8763-4

Printed in China

www.thomasnelson.com

09 10 11 12 13 [HH] 6 5 4 3 2 1

Contents

I wish you enough sun
to keep your attitude bright.

I wish you enough rain
to appreciate the sun more.

I wish you enough happiness
to keep your spirit alive.

I wish you enough pain
so that the smallest joys in life
appear much bigger.

I wish you enough gain
to satisfy your wanting.

I wish you enough loss
to appreciate all that you possess.

I wish you enough "Hellos"
to get you through the final "Good-bye."

introduction

I never really thought I'd spend as much time in airports as I do. I don't know why. I have always wanted to be famous, and I knew that would mean lots of travel. While I'm not exactly famous, I do see more than my share of airports.

I love them, and I hate them. I love them because of the people I get to watch. But that's also the same reason why I hate airports. It all comes down to hello and good-bye.

I have great difficulty saying good-bye. Even as I write this, I am experiencing that pounding sensation in my heart. If I am watching a farewell scene in a movie, I am affected so much that I often need to sit up and take a few deep breaths. So when faced with a challenge in my life, I have been known to go to our local airport and watch people say good-bye. I figure nothing that is happening to me at the time could be as bad as having to say good-bye.

Watching two people cling to each other, crying, and holding each other in that last embrace, makes me appreciate what I have even more. Seeing them finally pull apart—extending their arms until the tips of their fingers are the last to let go—is an image that stays in the forefront of my mind throughout the day.

On one of my recent business trips, when I arrived at the counter to check in, the woman said, "How are you today?"

I replied, "I am missing my wife already, and I haven't even said good-bye."

She then looked at my ticket and began to ask, "How long will you . . . Oh, my! You will only be gone three days!"

We both laughed. But my problem was that I still had to say good-bye to my wife.

I learn from good-bye moments too.

Recently I overheard a father and daughter in their last moments together. Her flight's departure had been announced, and they were standing near the security gate. They hugged tightly, and he said, "I love you. I wish you enough."

She in turn said, "Daddy, our life together has been more than enough. Your love is all I ever needed. I wish you enough too, Daddy."

They kissed, and she left. He walked over toward the window where I was seated. As I watched him standing there, I could see he wanted and needed to cry. I did not want to intrude on his privacy, but he welcomed me in by asking, "Did you ever say good-bye to someone knowing it would be forever?"

"Yes, I have," I replied, thinking back on those precious memories of the last few moments with my dad. Recognizing that his days were limited, I had taken the time to tell him face-to-face how much he meant to me and to express my love and appreciation for all he had done for me.

So I knew what this man experiencing.

"Forgive me for asking, but why is this a forever good-bye?" I asked.

"I am old, and she lives much too far away. I have challenges ahead, and the reality is, her next trip back will be for my funeral," he said.

"When you were saying good-bye, I heard you say, 'I wish you enough.' May I ask what that means?"

The man began to smile as he answered, "That's a wish that has been handed down from other generations. My parents used to say it to everyone." He paused for a moment and, looking up as if trying to remember it in detail, he smiled even more. "When we said, 'I wish you enough,' we were wanting the other person to have a life filled with just enough good things to sustain them." Then he turned toward me and shared the following as if he were reciting it from memory:

I wish you enough sun to keep your attitude bright.

I wish you enough rain to appreciate the sun more.

I wish you enough happiness to keep your spirit alive.

I wish you enough pain so that the smallest joys in life appear much bigger.

I wish you enough gain to satisfy your wanting.

I wish you enough loss to appreciate all that you possess.

I wish enough hellos to get you through the final good-bye.

Still smiling, but now with tears streaming, he turned and walked away.

My friends, I wish you enough!
Bob Perks

My grace is sufficient for you, for My strength is made perfect in weakness.

2 Corinthians 12:9

I wish you enough

sun

to keep your attitude

bright.

sun

We are drawn to eternal light. When the circumstances of our lives are gloomy, we are told to look on the bright side. In midwinter we long for the sunny days of spring and summer.

So, "I wish you enough sun" is a hopeful thing to want for someone.

Here I offer to you stories of hope that look at the brighter side of life or reflect a longing for brighter days ahead.

Anyone can see the sun on a sunny day, but sometimes our sunny moments come from the darkest places.

My friend . . .
I wish you enough sun to
keep your attitude bright.

FOR THE LORD GOD
IS A SUN AND SHIELD...

Psalm 84:11

The Attitude of the Flower

Change happens. Life goes on.

That thought came to me just the other day as I set out to gather all of the leaves that had fallen thus far on our property. Fall is an incredible time of change. The dying leaves turn wondrous colors, painting the world with their varying hues. In their death, we find beauty—if only for a short time. But what of the flowers?

Out on our deck we have four large flowerpots. Each year we fill them with a variety of flowers and plants. Usually all but a few hardy flowers wither and die with the first frost. We as humans know when it is time to say good-bye to the warmth and wonder of summer. We prepare ourselves for it. The trees do the same as they shut down their systems. Of course, the squirrels and other animals have been planning their retreat for weeks. But as for the flowers . . . those hardy ones . . . they keep right on growing, stretching up toward the light. No one ever told them not to. No one ever told them that they couldn't reach their full potential. They have a purpose that they must fulfill.

Even though the leaves are falling and the wind is growing chilly, I found fresh green leaves there in our four flowerpots, and at the end of each stem was new growth. Small buds of pink and red were curled over, not dying, but waiting, almost in a swing position, ready to spring out and stretch once again toward the sun. Sadly, I know that the snow will come and cover and freeze them in their ready position. Soon it will be too much even for these fighters. But they will keep trying until the end. That's what they are supposed to do. They were created to go on, to grow, and to bloom into forever. No one told them any different. They were created to be about growth and blooming, not hibernation or death. Much like each of us.

Who are you listening to? Who has told you that you can't become more? Who have you turned your life over to, allowing them to control your destiny? How have you redesigned your genetic structure to limit your full potential?

There are no seasons of frost and bitter cold that are strong enough to stop you. Only you can stop you. Yes, there may be times of slower growth—we live in an imperfect world, full of imperfect people. But when you find yourself withering, reconnect to the One who created winter and conquered death; begin growing again in that private place deep within your soul that always stretches toward the light.

Take on the attitude of the flower. For although it sees others dying all around it, it continues its mission with purpose and dignity, living to its fullness as determined by the One who created it.

We are told that there is a time to sow and a time to reap. A time to be born and a time to die (Ecclesiastes 3). Look at how much of your life is in your own hands. Work hard and reap the benefits. Live a healthy life and delay the inevitable. All the necessary resources are provided for you, except for the way you choose to think. Everything we need physically comes from the earth, but our thoughts are either our own or those that we choose to accept from others.

If flowers can continually strive toward their full potential, imagine then what greatness and beauty you have inside. If God has provided for the flowers to live so beautifully and completely, how much more can you do with the power and resources He has given you?

Keep reaching toward the sun.

LIFT YOUR EYES AND LOOK TO THE HEAVENS....

Isaiah 40:26 NIV

Weeding 101

I come from the dark ages. We didn't have weed whackers when I was a kid. I had to dig the weeds out from the cracks in the sidewalk—sometimes with a tool as crude as a screwdriver. So seeing this young guy brought back all those memories.

You see, I visited a local park today. I love to run away from telephones, faxes, beepers, and all those other electronic invaders to reclaim my sanity. Sometimes it even works. But most of the time, I end up thinking about all the things that I was trying to forget about by doing work. It's can be a lose-lose situation.

On this day, I was sitting on a bench at the edge of the lake. A young man walked up with a bucket filled with tools and a determined look on his face. He surveyed the pavement around him, which was cracked and filled with weeds.

"I don't know why I'm doing this," he said, half to himself and half to me. "They'll just be back in a few days."

"Where's your superpowered weed whacker?" I asked.

"We don't have enough to go around," he replied. "The older guys get to use them."

"I still don't understand why God made weeds to begin with," I said. "They grow over the beautiful stuff and choke out the flowers."

The young man then surprised me by smiling and saying, "But weeds are beautiful. One man's weeds are another man's flowers. And they are an example to anyone who wants to get ahead in life."

Right. Now this college boy is going to try to convince me that there's a lesson in the life of a weed. I see a lot of possibilities in life, but this one is going to take some convincing.

He went on to explain.

"The thing about weeds is they adapt to wherever they are. Have you ever seen a single weed growing in the middle of a parking lot? What are the odds that a weed would even find the tiny crack, root itself, and grow?" he asked. "And what about their ability to make a comeback? Did you ever pull up a weed and then, just days later, it's back again, bigger than ever? That's because its roots go deep. We can chop it off at the head, and it will come right back. People don't come back that quickly."

I sat quietly for once. He was making sense. Perhaps there was a life lesson in weeds.

The young man continued, "I've seen trees growing in the most unlikely places—even on the side of a steep rocky mountain. Do they serve a purpose way up there? They can't give us shade, but they become a home for birds. They prevent erosion. They have a purpose."

"Bloom where you are planted," I said.

"What?"

"It's a concept from the Bible. Everything you said is true. We always want to be somewhere else. We cry and moan about our circumstances and fall between those same cracks that weeds flourish in," I said.

"Where we are is where we should grow?" he asked.

"The difference between people and weeds is that we have what I call the gift of choice. We can choose to grow, sow, or go. Grow where you are with what you have. Sow your gifts and talents for future growth. Or go on to another environment more suitable for your needs," I said.

"The weed is pretty incredible, isn't it?" the young man said with a grin.

"Yes, and so are you, my friend. You've taught me a great lesson today," I said as I shook his hand.

"We both learned something. This has helped me decide what I want to take in college."

"Let me guess. Something to do with the environment," I said.

"Oh no! I hate the outdoors. I'm going into finance. I want to make it big so I can hire someone to pull my weeds for me."

He was kidding. He was kidding, right?

It's a funny place to be at this point in my life. When I was a kid, I learned from adults. Now that I am an adult, I'm learning from kids.

Never stop learning—or blooming.

I HAVE LEARNED IN WHATEVER STATE I AM, TO BE CONTENT.

Philippians 4:11

Look! You're a Star Already!

"It's the brightest one, Dad, isn't it?" the young boy asked.

Patting the boy's head, his father said, "It would have to be the brightest one to be my son's star."

The father was carrying on the tradition that had been handed down for generations. His own father had done the same thing for him when he was small. They were finding the boy's "Future Star."

"Everyone needs something to shoot for. So why not reach for the stars?" he explained.

Now this father believed in the power of that star just as much as his son did. Reflecting back on the day he had discovered his own "Future Star," he told his son, "From the moment your grandfather pointed out my star, my whole life changed."

"How, Dad?" the boy asked.

"I stopped looking down. I couldn't wait until the evening so that I could find it again. And the moment I spotted it, I knew everything was going to be all right. No matter what was wrong, my star gave me peace in my heart," he said.

"Does it really have power, Dad? I mean, can I break iron with it?" the child asked.

"No. It's not the kind of power that makes you big and strong like Superman. It's the kind of power that makes you the superhero of your own life. It's knowledge. It's belief. It's knowing that you can accomplish anything you put your mind to, if you only believe you can--and work very hard for it, of course."

"Why do we call it the 'Future Star'?" the child asked.

"This star is your guide," he answered. "You see, sailors have been guided by the stars for centuries. Poets and writers have written about them. Singers have sung about them. Dreamers and lovers have spent hours just watching them. That's how important they are. And one day you will become a bright and shining star."

"You mean up there in heaven?"

"Well, at first right here on earth. By believing in its light and in the One who made that light, by working for the goals you set for yourself, and by trusting in the talents you were given, you will become a star—a light to guide and inspire those around you."

"What about when it's cloudy, Dad? I won't be able to see my star then."

"Well, my son, that's what believing is all about. You don't have to see your star to know it's always there."

The young child sat for a moment. His father watched him, memorizing the details of the moment and knowing they would both remember it for a lifetime.

"So the star will always protect me?" the young child asked.

You can't find a moment better than this! the father thought to himself.

Turning to the boy, he asked, "Who did I tell you made the stars?"

"God?" the son replied.

"Yes," the father said. "And if God can create and take care of all these stars . . ."

"Then He can take care of me!" the boy interrupted with a smile.

"Ah, son," his father said as he knelt down in front of him. Taking the boy's small face in his hands, he kissed him. Tears of love and pride welled up in his eyes as he said, "Look! You're a star already!"

I believe in you!

HE COUNTS THE NUMBER OF THE STARS; HE CALLS THEM ALL BY NAME.

Psalm 147:4

I wish you enough

rain

to appreciate

the sun more.

rain

"Rainy days and Mondays always get me down." So the song goes, but this wish asks for rainy days.

Why?

Simply because the sunny days are so much more appreciated when they are interrupted by a little rain. If it never rained, we would never know the real joy of the sun. If everything went perfectly well all the time, we would become complacent and perhaps bored with our lives. We would begin to take life for granted.

So celebrate those times when the rainy days seem to spoil your fun. Run out and splash in it, just like when you were a child and a little rain was a welcome sight.

My friend...
I wish you enough rain to
appreciate the sun more.

AND WE KNOW THAT ALL THINGS
WORK TOGETHER FOR GOOD TO THOSE WHO
LOVE GOD, TO THOSE WHO ARE THE CALLED
ACCORDING TO HIS PURPOSE.

Romans 8:28

They Ran Through the Rain Believing

I listen. That's where my stories come from.

I speak. That's how I get to meet the most incredible people.

But sometimes just listening from afar is enough to fill my heart. I don't always need to say hello to bring a perfect stranger into my life. Conversations overheard can provide life lessons even more powerful than conversations we are actually a part of.

Not long ago I had a brief encounter that filled my day—and my heart—to capacity. If only they knew the gift they gave me:

She must have been six years old, this beautiful brown-haired, freckle-faced image of innocence. Her mom could have posed for a Norman Rockwell painting. Not that she was old-fashioned. Her brown hair was ear length with enough curl to appear natural. She had on a pair of tan shorts and a light blue knit shirt. Her sneakers were white with blue trim.

She looked like . . . a mom.

It was pouring outside. The kind of rain that gushes over the tops of rain gutters, in such a hurry to hit the earth that it has no time to flow down the spout. Drains in the nearby parking lot were filled to capacity, leaving huge puddles to lake around the parked cars.

We all stood there under the awning, just inside the door of the Wal-Mart. We waited, some patiently, others aggravated because nature had messed up their hurried day.

I am always mesmerized by rainfall. I get lost in the sound and the sight of the heavens washing away the dirt and dust of the world. Memories of running, splashing carefree as a child come pouring in as a welcome reprieve from the worries of my day.

Her voice was so sweet as it broke the hypnotic trance we were all caught in.

"Mom, let's run through the rain," she said.

"What?" her mother asked.

"Let's run through the rain!" she repeated.

"No, honey. We'll wait until it slows down a bit," Mom replied.

The young child waited another minute and then repeated her statement. "Mom . . . let's run through the rain."

"We'll get soaked if we do," said Mom.

"No, we won't, Mom. That's not what you said this morning," insisted the young girl as she tugged at her mother's arm.

"This morning? When did I say we could run through the rain and not get wet?"

"Don't you remember? When you were talking to Daddy about his cancer, you said, 'If God can get us through this, He can get us through anything!'"

The entire crowd stopped dead silent. You couldn't hear anything except the splashing of the rain. We all stood quietly, waiting to see what would happen.

The mother paused and thought for a moment about what she would say. Now some mothers would laugh it off and scold the child for being silly. Some might even ignore what she had said. But this was a moment of affirmation in a young child's life. A time when innocent trust could be nurtured so that it would bloom into faith.

"Honey, you are absolutely right. Let's run through the rain. If God lets us get wet, well, maybe we just needed washing," Mom said.

Then off they ran. We all stood watching, smiling and laughing as they darted past the cars and, yes, through the puddles. They held their shopping bags over their heads just in case.

They got soaked. But they were followed by a few believers who screamed and laughed like children all the way to their cars . . . perhaps inspired by the little girl's faith and trust.

I want to believe that somewhere down the road in life, that mother will find herself reflecting back on these moments they spent together, captured like pictures in the scrapbook of her cherished memories. Perhaps when she watches proudly as her daughter graduates . . . or as her daddy walks her down the aisle on her wedding day.

She will laugh again. Her heart will beat a little faster. Her smile will tell the world they love each other. But only two people will share that precious moment when they ran through the rain believing that God would get them through.

And, yes, I did.
I ran through the rain.
I got wet.
I guess I needed washing.

WASH ME, AND I SHALL BE WHITER THAN SNOW.

Psalm 51:7

He'll Be Back

She wouldn't let go. Most times he'd fuss about it. But this time he seemed to understand. He enjoyed the embrace just as he had so many times before. There were moments, in fact, when he longed for her tender touch. But he could never admit it.

There will be times ahead when he would wish he hadn't let go.

He was just about to close his suitcase when she walked in. He expected this to be a difficult parting. But he didn't realize how difficult.

"Now don't forget to feed Freddie on time," he said as he slowly pushed back away from her embrace. "You know how crazy he gets if he's not fed on time. He'll bark until you do."

She remained silent.

"Look, here's the phone number where I can be reached until I get my own phone. There will always be someone at this number in case you really need to reach me," he said.

"How many years have you been a part of my life?" she asked, just needing to hear him say it.

"Almost twenty."

"So you can understand why this is so very difficult for me, right?"

"It isn't easy for me either," he told her as he turned and placed his arms around her shoulders. "You have always been there. I never had a worry in the world knowing you were there."

"What am I going to do with all the silence in this house? How will I sleep, wondering where you are, how you are doing?" she said.

A car horn beeped from the street below.

It was time. This suitcase was the last piece to be packed.

"Beep! Beep!" The horn sounded again, urging him to hurry.

They headed out the door and, as he exited the room, she turned slowly and paused for a moment in the doorway. A thousand memories came flooding through her mind. A million moments of happiness and anguish overflowed her heart.

Then she caught up with him at the bottom of the stairs.

He grabbed a backpack and walked toward the front door. As he opened it slowly, he stopped halfway and said, "I know I must have said this a thousand times, but you do know how much I love you, don't you?"

She fell forward into his arms and without shedding a single tear, just as she promised herself, she said, "Yes, you've proven that a thousand times."

He kissed her on the cheek and, as he headed down the sidewalk, he turned halfway and blew her a kiss.

The car pulled away slowly, and she watched until she could see him no more.

Without hesitation she turned and ran back to his room. Throwing herself on the bed, she cried so hard that her eyes felt as if they were drowning.

Rolling to her side, she glanced again at what was left of his.

There in the corner, still hanging on the wall, was Joey's lucky bat and glove. High upon the shelf stood the trophy he had won his senior year in swimming. Stacks of boxes contained his baseball card collection, and on the wall just above his desk was an empty spot where a picture had hung.

He had insisted on taking it with him. You see, he played the tough guy here. By all worldly standards, he needed to be a man. By all rights, he was still a boy. But that picture would be his connection to home over the next four years. Hung in just the right place in his dorm, it would remind him of his roots. One glimpse at just the right time during those late-night hours cramming for the finals would give him that extra push he needed. He would be able to see himself as a part of something bigger than all the world.

Family.

In the split-second flash of a camera, all the inspiration he would ever need had been captured.

It was his high-school graduation. That's him in the middle with Mom and Dad on either side. The smiles tell it all. They were so very proud of him. Now he is off to claim his place in life. It's something he has to accomplish. He has a purpose greater than the diploma he'll get. You see, Dad died shortly after that moment, and Mom has been working two jobs ever since to make sure he'd have this chance.

If this were a movie, the script would call for a split screen. There, on the left, Mom is seen sitting at his desk back home. Slowly reaching up to where the picture once hung, she gently rubs her hand across the surface. "Oh, Joey, we are so very proud of you!"

To the right on the screen, at that very same moment, Joey reaches into the backpack placed carefully by his feet in the car. He pulls out the photo and, running his hand slowly across the glass, says, "Mom, Dad, I'll make you proud."

The screen fades to black.
Life is in constant transition, moving forward,
moving on.
But love is stronger than distance or time.
He'll be back.

BUT THOSE WHO WAIT ON THE LORD
SHALL RENEW THEIR STRENGTH;
THEY SHALL MOUNT UP WITH
WINGS LIKE EAGLES,
THEY SHALL RUN AND NOT BE WEARY,
THEY SHALL WALK AND NOT FAINT.

Isaiah 40:31

Feeling Low?

Yes, I have those days. You know, when things just aren't as right as they should be. Oh, they are right with the world. Just not with me.

So I struggle through them just like you do. I'm happy to report that I have made it through every one of those days. Even the really hard ones. The ones when the world seemed to hate me, and everything in it seemed ugly.

I am learning that my perception becomes my reality.

Then there are those other days when there really isn't much of a challenge, but just enough to make me feel low.

I was having one of those low days recently. I knew I'd get through it. I knew I'd get over it.

Still, I was right in the middle of it when I decided to walk around my yard.

I paused at the small pond and watched the nine fish and two frogs that I love so much. Hoping they would bring a little smile to my face, I stooped down to "talk" with my frogs.

Both of them took off, adding to my gloom.

"Even the frogs don't want to see me," I whined.

I stood up and headed for the bird feeders. Oftentimes if I stand there long enough and still enough, the small birds will come down and feast on the treats I supply them with every day.

Not today. Not one.

The picture was getting darker. Not because the world was out to shun me—the world was just being the world. And I, not appreciating that, chose to only see what I wanted to see . . . proof that I was not worthy.

I was about to turn around and head back into the house to wallow in my self-pity when I caught a glimpse of the sunflowers my wife had planted in our small vegetable garden.

I was stunned. "Look at what happened!" I said out loud. "This isn't fair at all!"

You see, each year early in spring, my wife and I plant several sunflower seeds. We have tried to grow them for years, but somewhere along the way they always die. One year we managed to grow a single, wonderful flower. But as soon as it opened, a hungry squirrel pounced on it, bending it to the ground, and devoured most of it. But this year, five had survived!

So as soon as the sunflowers started growing, I had placed netting around and over the entire garden. The battle to protect the sunflowers was on.

These sunflowers soon became enormous. Between ten and twelve feet high. That's right—ten and twelve feet!

And now, on this gloomy and depressing day, the first and tallest one reached for the sun, opened its bloom, and . . . slumped over.

I felt so sorry for it.

I walked up to the fence to tell it so.

"Oh, how sad," I said. "I did all that I could to protect you, and now . . . now I know exactly how you feel."

That was when I heard these words: "I did feel low until you walked up. I was looking at the others, and I tried to lift up my head, but I couldn't. I was feeling terrible until you arrived."

"Me? What did I do?" I asked the flower.

"When my head was so low and I couldn't see the sun, you came, and I realized that as low as I felt, you were looking up to me."

She was right. The flower felt low, but there was someone lower. As tough as things have been in my life, I realized that there was always someone who has it tougher.

Even in my most challenging moments, days, weeks, months, or years, I can always find someone I can lift up.

Life is such that in your lowest times, you can always reach down to help someone else. In doing so, you touch one life and change two.

Feeling low? Reach lower.

THE LORD IS MY STRENGTH AND MY SHIELD;
MY HEART TRUSTED IN HIM,
AND I AM HELPED;
THEREFORE MY HEART GREATLY REJOICES,
AND WITH MY SONG I WILL PRAISE HIM.

Psalm 28:7

She Likes Her Days Cloudy

Sometimes being self-employed is difficult. I often long for conversations with co-workers over a cup of coffee. Or even a midmorning meeting held in the boardroom to discuss company growth. Many days I wake up longing for an opportunity, and then I find myself right where I'm supposed to be, connecting with a total stranger. Perhaps a messenger with a story for me to share.

Today was that kind of day. I headed out to fulfill my longing for pancakes, the light fluffy kind that never seem to fill, but always satisfy. It was a comfortable fall morning and was actually an uneventful one right through breakfast. Then, just as I got up to leave, an older woman, perhaps in her late sixties or early seventies, stood up in front of me and slowly headed to the register. Lately, I've been trying to slow myself down to let the world catch up with me, so this was a needed lesson in patience. She fumbled for her bill and the exact change, and she chatted with the young cashier. I was in no hurry. At last I paid my bill and headed for the door, while she was still fidgeting with her purse. As I turned around at the door, I spotted her approach and decided to wait to hold the door for her.

"Thank you, young man," she said.

Well, being called "young man" was certainly worth the wait!

As we exited the building, she declared this to be a beautiful day, and I agreed. "Except," she said, "there are no clouds in the sky. I love clouds."

Most people consider a cloudy day to be dreary and depressing. But this wonderful lady loved the clouds. As I was soon to discover, she takes photos of them through her picture window overlooking the lake. She has collected hundreds of them. Especially those incredible moments at sunset.

I needed her today. I had just commented to my wife about my lack of friends to share time with during the day, so God had sent me one. I could sense that she too was looking for a conversation. She never stopped talking. She had this incredible ability to connect stories one to another. The clouds reminded her of the beautiful yard she has and the wedding receptions held on her property in absolute perfect weather each time. Of course, that thought brought to mind the memory of her husband, who—shortly after attending their daughter's wedding—died from cancer. He was a miracle of sorts. As sick as he was, he walked his daughter down the aisle and even danced the first dance. Then, just a few short years later, her daughter, her beautiful daughter of thirty-nine years, died from ovarian cancer.

We spoke for nearly twenty minutes in the parking lot without even sharing our names until I thanked her and offered her my business card.

Gerri—I'm guessing short for Geraldine—touched my life. I told her she was my gift for today. She nearly started to cry.

So today I learned about clouds. There are clouds that darken our soul, like the loss of a daughter and husband. Then there are clouds that brighten our view of the world, ever changing right before our eyes in the form of a sunset.

Stop today and look for the clouds in your life. The ones that bring joy and a smile to your face.

By the way, at the end of the twenty-minute conversation, the perfectly clear blue sky was suddenly transformed by the most incredible hand-drawn streams of white puffy clouds.

"They look like birds," she said and smiled.

They did. I let my heart take flight, and my soul thanked God for clouds.

I can't wait for tomorrow. They are forecasting . . . partly cloudy skies.

YOUR MERCY, O LORD, IS IN THE HEAVENS; YOUR FAITHFULNESS REACHES TO THE CLOUDS.

Psalm 36:5

I wish you enough

happiness

to keep
your spirit

alive.

happiness

How many people do you know who are never happy?

It seems that all of their lives they have been chasing after happiness, but never quite grabbing hold of it.

The sad part about it is they have actually chosen not to be happy. It isn't that happiness has eluded them; it is that they just never found joy in the everyday things that others delight in. Their expectations may have been based on getting certain things or reaching certain goals, rather than the stuff of life.

The following stories are happy stories, although some are stories of sadness that have happy endings. Like Neil Diamond's song "I Believe in Happy Endings," perhaps we must learn to find happiness in all of life's challenges.

My friend...
    I wish you enough happiness to
       keep your spirit alive.

THESE THINGS I HAVE SPOKEN TO YOU,
THAT MY JOY MAY REMAIN IN YOU, AND
THAT YOUR JOY MAY BE FULL.

John 15:11

Appland Life

I stood on a large rock at the back of the hotel, high atop a hill overlooking a golf course. From my vantage point I could see for miles. From off to my right, I heard the faint sounds of an approaching train. To my left was the greatest show on earth. No, not the circus. The sunset.

I had been in a hurry to get settled into my room for the evening. Having just traveled about five hours, I was tired and hungry. I rushed out the back door and planned on heading to the mall across the street. During my previous visit here, I remembered that they had not one, but two, Chinese restaurants. I love chicken fried rice and wonton soup.

But it all had to wait. It was calling me again.

Just as I reached for my keys, I looked up and saw the great possibilities in the patterns that were forming off in the distance. I argued with my growling stomach and my Mickey Mouse watch that this wouldn't take very long. But a good sunset from beginning to end often does.

I discovered a huge boulder that was perfectly placed at the corner of the property, right on the edge of the hill. Some landscape designer had most likely charged the hotel owners a bundle to place the boulder there—for it served as a focal point for people to gather as they toured the property and the sales manager pointed out the nearby golf course and tennis club.

Yes, others had been there before me, perhaps breathing in the fresh air and soaking up the last rays of sunshine.

But today I was happy to have this front-row seat all to myself.

About a half mile away, the approaching train passed by the remnants of a previously occupied factory and then hauled its dozen or more flat cars through the wooded backdrop of the ninth hole. While seated in my hot tub at home, I often wave at planes flying overhead as I wonder where the passengers are headed. It seemed appropriate to do the same for the trainmen. I knew they couldn't see me, but it still mattered to me.

As I watched, the sun began its final descent, painting the clouds and sending golden beams of light high into the sky. The brightness of the sunset created a silhouette of the trees and buildings before me. I turned away for a moment, so that even I cast a long shadow across the parking lot, making me feel bigger than I am.

Then the finale.

I heard a voice inside me. It was that childish prankster from my past that taunts me with "Dare ya!" and "Bet you won't do it!"

So I did. I didn't care who might be looking. I applauded as if I had just seen the final performance of *Cats* on Broadway. I even yelled "All right!" and "That's a keeper!"

It was over. I slowly turned wondering if anyone saw me. But no one was there. Someone should have noticed. How sad it was. They were probably having pizza somewhere. But they lost and I gained.

They would have at least had a good laugh at the man who applauded life. Or perhaps they would have joined me. Maybe next time.

When was the last time life was so exciting that joy and happiness burst out and you just had to stand up and applaud?

Here is my challenge to you. Tomorrow when you wake up, jump out of bed and applaud. Whistle and yell, "All right!" and "This is a keeper!" And then just wait until you see how your day turns out.

I dare ya! Double dare ya!

BE STILL, AND KNOW THAT I AM GOD.

—Psalm 46:10

If You Only Knew

"The problem is we just don't know," he said.

"We just don't know what?" I asked.

"We just don't know what is expected of us."

"From friends and family?" I asked.

"No. From God."

I didn't think that to be true. I believe there are clear guidelines set for each of us.

"Isn't there a rule book? I think we call it the Bible?" I said smiling.

He gave me one of those looks that my wife gives me when I am being sarcastic.

"I'm not talking about rules. I'm not talking about guidelines for how we should live," he said.

"Then what?" I asked.

"I don't believe we know what God sees in us," he said. "I don't believe we know the potential, the possibilities, the facts, and the truth we hold inside ourselves."

I was stunned. I mean, I really never thought about it that way. He was right. I believe most of us see our faith as a set of rules and regulations. Like a "how to" book on life or an instruction manual for operating within our faith.

"God is telling us so much more, but we aren't listening," he continued. "In fact, I believe those outside any kind of faith see faith as too limiting. Many faith-filled believers don't even realize what they have."

He may be right.

"Faith is seeing a stream, but believing in the ocean," I said.

"Yes!" he shouted with excitement.

I love conversations like this. I need to hear what I believe to be true. God has given us instructions not just on how to live, but on how to become all He sees in us. Words not of possibilities, but of fact.

"If we only knew," he said.

How powerful that is. Faith is not just possibilities. To have faith says, "This is what I know," not "This is what I think I know."

Faith is not "What do I believe?" but "What do I know to be true?"

The very second we turn believing into knowing, we instantly become all that God sees in us.

> If I only knew love . . . I would be more loving.
> If I only knew hope . . . I would be hopeful.
> If I only knew I could not fail . . . I would be successful.
> If I only knew happiness . . . sadness would not have a place in my life.
> If I only knew joy . . . joy would be given to all who knew me.
> If I only knew peace . . . there would be no war.

To know is to see what God sees in you.
To see what God sees in you is to
acknowledge God in your life.

Faith is . . . if you only knew.

NOW FAITH IS THE SUBSTANCE OF THINGS HOPED FOR, THE EVIDENCE OF THINGS NOT SEEN.

Hebrews 11:1

The Way I See It

Stars play a significant role in my life. It's the heavens I turn to when I am lost and feeling unimportant. But perhaps, in the scheme of things, it might be the worst thing I could do.

Think about it. If you want to look and feel taller, would you head to New York City and stand next to the Empire State Building? If you thought that God had given you a beautiful singing voice, would you want to sing a duet with Andrea Bocelli?

You would probably say, "No! Of course not! It's best to keep things in perspective. You should know your place in life, your limits."

The Empire State Building would make you feel small and insignificant, and Bocelli would make you sound like you're gargling with sand.

So along that line of thinking, seeking significance by looking into the vastness of the universe would certainly have the opposite result. Most people would feel like a speck of dust compared to the billions of stars and millions of galaxies yet uncharted.

But there, my friend, is where they are wrong.

You see, the key here is perspective. It's how you see something, and how I see something. In my talks I refer to "The Way It Is" model. Two different viewpoints and the reality that somewhere in the middle of those opposing thoughts is "The Way It Is."

I stand next to the Empire State Building so that I can see how big things can be. At one time, someone thought that building to be an impossibility. Yet I have stood on top of that impossibility, and it was awesome!

I proudly sing along with Andrea Bocelli too. First of all, I do sing with him every day as I travel by car or as I work around the house. I may not have the purity of such a well-trained voice, but I have and do sing professionally. Would I ever turn down the honor of actually singing with him? No way! I'd go for it. Being the professional he is, he would most likely be easy on me. He'd permit me to sound good.

By some standards or perspectives, Bocelli himself would be labeled an impossibility because of his blindness. You see, once again someone would see limits instead of potential.

His success tells me there are no limits.

As does the night sky.

I'll be the first to admit that whenever I really ponder the heavens, it takes my breath away. I have seen photos of stars, planets, and galaxies that were taken far beyond what anyone would have imagined possible.

In life we think things must have a beginning and an end. Yet, in contrast, we stare into the heavens and use them to help us define the words *forever* and *infinity*.

You would think that seeing my life as significant in this endless universe may be a challenge. But as I see it, you and I are more significant than any element of the universe, known or unknown. For we were created to reign over all of this. We have the capacity to question it and the ability to comprehend it.

A galaxy may exist for millions of years and, then for whatever reason be destroyed without having much of an impact on the universe as a whole. But you and I have the ability to change the world we live in. A single act or a lifetime of dedication to humanity sends a ripple into time, forever, and into infinity.

If you have faith then you know that there is nothing about you that is by chance. You were created on purpose and with purpose. But you were also given the gift of choice. You can choose to either feel small or tall. You can choose to see possibilities or limitations. You can be overwhelmed by the struggles of life, or you can choose to be overcome with the joy of the One who created life.

Tonight go out into the darkness and look into the heavens. They are there not to make you feel small, but to show you there are no limits.

You were created to give God glory for it.

THE HEAVENS DECLARE THE GLORY OF GOD; AND THE FIRMAMENT SHOWS HIS HANDIWORK.

Psalm 19:1

She Didn't Have to Say a Word

Scattered all around me in the restaurant are families having dinner, friends catching up on the latest news, business meetings, and people like me just there to relax. And, of course, great conversation.

Except in the booth across from me. Silence.

When I first sat down, there were two men sitting together quietly. One man appeared to be in his thirties. He was dressed in some old work clothes and still wearing his baseball cap. I would guess the other man was about eighty or so. He had the most incredible face. Its lines and creases gave him character. His white hair was messy from wearing the stocking cap that he held on top of the table. He wore one of those red plaid shirt jackets that you might see on a construction worker. Heavy enough to keep you warm while you're moving about, but not too bulky to limit your movement.

But he didn't look like he was going anywhere. Neither was their conversation.

"Boy, I really worked up a hunger today, Pop," said the younger man. "All that shoveling and sweeping the snow will do that."

"Yeah, this snow is somethin'," replied the old man.

Silence followed for the longest time.

Suddenly I heard the young man say, "Here they come," as he pointed toward the doorway.

He almost looked relieved. Somebody who would join in and help get this conversation going.

It appeared to me that the two people who joined them were a mother and her teenage daughter, the old man's grandchild perhaps. The woman sat next to the younger man, while the older man stood up to let the grandchild slide in.

"Hello, Dad. Good to see you!" said the woman as she sat down.

"Yep!" the old man replied.

Silence. Even longer than before.

"I feel real good," the old man announced proudly.

"Oh, you look good, Pop," the younger man said. And the other two agreed.

Silence.

Pop excused himself. "Gotta go to the bathroom. It happens a lot when you're old," he said.

As soon as he was out of sight, the younger man said, "I don't know what to say to him. We just sit here looking at each other. He never talks."

"I know what you mean. But what do you say?" the woman added.

"He's old. What do you talk about with an old man?" the granddaughter chimed in.

Oh no. Here I go, I thought. I can't just sit here and listen to this. I'm going to say something, swallow hard, and wait to see if they tell me it's none of my business.

"Ask him about his childhood," I said as I continued eating.

"What? Pardon me? Were you talking to us, sir?" the woman asked.

"Yes. It's really not my business, I know. But do you realize what he has to offer you? Can you even imagine what this man has seen in his lifetime? He most likely has answers to problems you haven't even discovered as problems in your life. He's a gold mine!" I said.

Silence again.

"Look, talk to him about his childhood. Ask him what the snows were like back then. He'll have a million stories to share. He's not talking because no one is asking," I told them.

Just then he came walking around the corner.

"Oh, boy! I feel much better now. You know I haven't been goin' good in a while," the old man told them.

They all turned and looked at me. I shrugged my shoulders. Okay. So old people also talk about the facts of life. And going or not going is a major thing when you're old. You take the good with the bad.

After a long silence the young girl said, "PawPaw, when you were a kid, were the snows this bad?"

"Honey, this is nothing like the snows we had when I was a kid. Did I ever tell you about the snowstorm that covered my house?" he asked.

"No, Pop. I don't think I've heard that one myself," said the younger man.

So for the next twenty minutes, the old man was in his glory. At one point he even stood up to show them how high the one snowdrift was. Throughout the entire meal, everyone chimed in with more questions. They laughed, and he lit up like he was on stage, and the play he was acting in was his own life story.

Just as I was about to leave I heard the old man say, "You have no idea what this has meant to me. All these years I never thought you were even interested in what I had to say."

"Oh . . . well . . . I guess we just didn't think you wanted to talk," the woman said.

"Well, nobody bothered to ask me anything. I just figured I was boring or somethin'. It's been a tough life, you know. Ever since MaMa died, I really had nothing to say."

He paused for a moment. I could see him nervously wringing his rough, life-worn hands together.

"You see, she and I were like a song. I made the music and she . . . she was the words," he said.

Like tough guys of his time are supposed to do, he held back any visible emotion, just sniffled a bit and wiped his eye as he said, "No sense talkin' if you ain't got the words."

As I got up to leave, I looked again at their table. I saw the young girl wave and smile at me as she put her arm around PawPaw's shoulders.

She didn't have to say a word.
She'd found a gold mine.

A WORD FITLY SPOKEN IS LIKE APPLES OF GOLD
IN SETTINGS OF SILVER.

Proverbs 25:11

I wish you enough

pain

so that the
smallest joys in life appear

much
bigger.

pain

"No pain, no gain!"

"I wish you pain" seems like a sadistic thing to wish someone. Pain is something you'd wish on your worst enemy. But pain falls into that same category as rain in your life.

Both pain and rain help us grow.

It takes both the positive and negative to charge a battery.

These stories are painful reminders of how delicate life really can be.

My friend...
I wish you enough pain so that the
smallest joys in life appear much bigger.

GOD WILL WIPE AWAY EVERY TEAR FROM
THEIR EYES; THERE SHALL BE NO MORE DEATH,
NOR SORROW, NOR CRYING. THERE SHALL BE
NO MORE PAIN, FOR THE FORMER THINGS
HAVE PASSED AWAY.

Revelation 21:4

All She Had Was a Broken Heart

She walked into the room, and his eyes lit up. She didn't have to say a word; simply being there was proof enough that she loved him. They had both lost someone they loved. So this day of all days was a difficult one. She wanted to make this work. She was hurt, lonely, and afraid. It wasn't supposed to be this way.

But the fact was, he knew how she felt. There was obvious pain in his heart too. So the one thing that strengthened their love for each other was heartache, the most sorrowful kind.

Their eyes locked. He smiled, and she responded. He had a special way of bringing a smile to her face. It was the little things he did that never failed to touch her heart. And don't we all know that the essence of true love and commitment is in the little things?

She stood there in the doorway, and he motioned to her to sit next to him. Not trusting the childish grin he now had on his face, she hesitated for a moment, but gave in. She always did.

She sat at the far end of the couch teasing him. He quickly responded by sliding right next to her. She laughed, and he knew it was all right. He seemed to be fumbling for just the right words. There was an awkward moment of silence between them. Making an effort to calm his nerves, she reached over and held his hand. He looked at her with a grateful smile and squeezed her hand in return.

They looked at each other again, somehow knowing that this was a difficult time for both of them.

Then, suddenly, he reached behind a pillow that had been placed strategically nearby. He pulled out a large red envelope and nervously handed it to her.

She snapped back with a look of surprise. She really hadn't expected this.

"Wait, this goes with it," he said, and he handed her a small box, perfectly wrapped in white tissue paper covered with hearts and flowers.

She couldn't believe this was happening. *How could he have pulled this off? And why?*

"Now," he said, "read the card."

In great anticipation, she ripped open the envelope without hesitating. She wanted desperately to see what he had to say to her.

It read as follows:

> I know that this isn't easy for you. It has been a tough year for both of us.
> I know that Valentine's Day is a special day for people in love.
> I am sure that you would rather be out at a fancy dinner, I'm sorry.
> But I want you to know that . . . I love you.
>
> I know that valentines are supposed to get chocolate.
> So I went to the store today to buy some for you. I got the last piece.
> I told the clerk it was just perfect.

She stopped for a moment and looked at him. Her eyes sparkled in the light as tears formed in each corner. He knew he had done the right thing.

Slowly, she unwrapped the box, careful not to rip the paper, for she was sure that this was a keeper, a moment she would not ever forget.

Removing the lid, she found inside a chocolate heart, broken into pieces along with a note:

The lady said all she had left was a broken heart. I told her so did we.
I am so sorry that Dad left us, Mom.
But I just wanted you to know that we still have each other.

Happy Valentine's Day.
    Love,
      Your son,
      Adam

What better love on Valentine's Day than the love of a mother and child.

LOVE . . . BEARS ALL THINGS, BELIEVES
ALL THINGS, HOPES ALL THINGS, ENDURES
ALL THINGS. LOVE NEVER FAILS.

1 Corinthians 13:4 – 8

Hanging On by a Thread

A friend of mine is desperate. He told me he is hanging on by a thread.

I believe we are at that crossing point in the autumn season. Many of the leaves have already fallen. The beautiful, radiant colors that decorated the hillsides have now turned brown. Although a ride in the countryside is still breathtaking, the colors have lost a little of their luster.

That is how my friend sees his life. His once sparkling, bubbly personality is much like the leaves that have reached their max and now just hang there waiting to fall. My friend is just barely hanging on.

Hearing my friend speak so dimly about the most precious thing we have—life—just sends me into a sadness I haven't experienced since I, too, was depressed enough to want to die.

Oh, he really doesn't want to die. But he is holding a funeral for that vibrant spirit that once lived inside of him. He thinks it's dying. He wants to bury it. But you see that's the problem. It is buried. Buried inside him, beneath layers of doubt and foolish thoughts of failure. He's smothered it to the point where it, too, is hanging on by a thread.

But this is what happens in life.

He's telling me his story over the phone yesterday just as I am looking out the window toward my back yard. It's covered with leaves. I hate raking leaves. This will sound terrible, but I usually wait until all or most of the leaves have fallen and the great autumn winds have swept across my property. That's right. I'm hoping that most of those leaves blow away onto someone else's land. It's not as bad as it sounds. The guy across the street needs the exercise more than I do.

Well, here I am having this conversation about life and my friend's failing marriage. He believes his wife isn't faithful to him. In fact, he knows it. She speaks about some guy named Allan in her sleep. And there have been others before him. But my friend loves his wife so much that through the years he has internalized his pain. That is until now. Now he has lost his will, his energy.

Just as he tells me he is hanging on by a thread, a sudden gust of wind passes by, and the leaves on the tree outside begin to fall like snow. It really is a remarkable sight. As quickly as it started, the wind suddenly stops. There, hanging from a branch, is this leaf. Suspended in midair. From my vantage point, I think for sure it must be supported by something. It isn't.

I go downstairs, still listening to my friend rehash his long list of why his life is so bad. I walk into the driveway and now, standing underneath the leaf, I am totally confused. It is attached to nothing. It is just there. So it must be caught in a spider's web. But from where I stand, there isn't even the glimmer of a web. As if by magic, this leaf has halted its journey in midair.

"Bill, there's a leaf hanging here in midair," I say.

"What?"

"A leaf that was supposed to hit the ground has suddenly stopped and is just dangling there," I tell him.

"So?"

"That's your answer. Think about that leaf. Somewhere up there on a higher branch, this leaf spent its entire life. In fact, you could say it's been there since birth. Growing up there was awesome. All through its life it had the best of everything. It was surrounded by family and friends.

"It's been through a lot too. The storms that shook its branches, the lightning that struck down a nearby tree, and the small insects that ripped apart so many other leaves—these experiences were all devastating. But it survived.

"Then one day, it started to go through some changes. The kind of changes that life brings. It began to feel old and withered. Its beautiful color started to turn, and it began to lose its grip. Then one day it fell earthward. It had given up all hope of holding onto the lifeblood that kept it fed, strong, and healthy.

"But on the way to the fall, a simple invisible thread caught it. As if to say, 'Not yet, my friend. Not yet.'

"Now here it is. In the midair. And I believe that leaf is having a second birth. Yes, in spite of the fact that it appears old and dried up. In spite of the fact that the source of all of its joy and happiness just let it go without explanation. A net, an invisible thread of hope captured it on the way down.

"I believe that leaf has had a change in attitude. I believe that leaf is grateful. I believe that leaf believes in second chances. I believe that right where it is, it is thinking, 'Life isn't over yet. Look at all of the others lying down there. They gave up. I may not be way up where I started, but the view from here isn't bad at all.'"

There is silence on the phone. He doesn't say a word for a few minutes. Finally I say, "Do you understand what this leaf is telling us?"

"Yes, I do."

"Bill, this leaf is hanging on by a thread. For some reason, it didn't hit the ground today. That thread that you spoke of. Where did it come from? Who put it there? What's it made of?" I ask.

"Faith. Will. God," he says quietly.

"So let's acknowledge that you have fallen a bit lower than you were before. So what are you going to do about it?"

"Enjoy the view?"

"No, only leaves can do that. You are a man of faith, will, and God. That leaf is still going to fall. It can't do anything about it, but you can. It has no choice about what it is, what it can do, or what will happen to it. You do. You can choose to do or be anything you want to," I tell him.

"So what should I do now?" he asks.

"Hang up the phone and come over here," I said.

About fifteen minutes later, he arrives. I am standing in my driveway with two rakes. We spend the next hour and a half gathering leaves into bags. We hardly speak at all. We hardly put a dent in the mess.

"There, my friend, that's what you need to do. Clean up your life," I say.

"But we're not finished. There's more," he observes.

Pointing up into the tree, I say, "There will always be more. Life is just that way. Look, that leaf is still hanging there."

Then Bill walks into my house and a few minutes later walks out with a piece of thread and a small stepladder. Standing on the very top step, he reaches up and grabs the suspended leaf. I watch in amazement as he ties one end of the thread to the leaf and the other to the branch.

"There. Now it will be more secure. It's not where it used to be. But it's hanging on by a thread with a little help from a friend," he says.

Then he walks over and shakes my hand, and says. "Thanks, my friend, for the thread."

I just say, "Hang in there!"

COME TO ME, ALL YOU WHO LABOR AND ARE
HEAVY LADEN, AND I WILL GIVE YOU REST.
TAKE MY YOKE UPON YOU AND LEARN FROM
ME, FOR I AM GENTLE AND LOWLY IN HEART,
AND YOU WILL FIND REST FOR YOUR SOULS.

Matthew 11:28−29

Forgiven?

It's become a ritual for me. Once a year, I go through the closet in my mind and force myself to accept God's forgiveness.

I guess that sounds like I've done a lot of bad things in my life. Well, some. But mostly I deal with the bad memories of things I've done. Let me explain.

There are things in our lives that we say or do that perhaps at some level we regret. The ones we deal with immediately oftentimes get buried or forgotten completely because we deal with them emotionally and maybe even ask for forgiveness right then and there.

But there are issues in many lives that never go away. Little hurtful actions on our part are sometimes triggered by current events. On those days when we are depressed or disappointed in the way things are going in our lives, we methodically return to that mental file we keep handy. You know, the one you call upon every time you criticize yourself and subconsciously reinforce the negative images that hold you back.

"Boy, am I stupid!"

"I'm just no good at this!"

"I'm such a klutz!"

"If it weren't for bad luck, I'd have no luck at all!"

Sound familiar? Most of us think like this every day.

But yesterday was my day of redemption. I normally hang an American flag in front of my home. It's up through most of the good weather months, not just on national holidays. I replace my flag faithfully as it becomes faded and torn. I need a new one this year. I'm proud to be an American. But don't get me started on that. I'll have to pull out the soapbox and sing "God Bless America!"

But on this one special day, I hang a flag that I struggle with. It is my Easter flag that bears a golden cross and the word *Forgiven* on it.

The first time I placed it in the holder, I couldn't look up at the passing cars. In my mind, every person I had ever wronged or hurt in some way was driving by at that moment. I could hear them say, "Who does he think he is? I haven't forgiven him!"

The odd thing is that for weeks after we hang it, people ask us where they can get one. They, too, want the world to know that they are forgiven.

This year, as I prepared to hang the flag, I carried with it all of my negative self-images inside it. Then, as the flag unfurled, I watched the wind blow them away.

The wind that took them away is, I believe, the last breath of Jesus Christ as He died upon the cross so that I could hang that flag with my head held high this year.

Some people may not yet have forgiven me. But the One who matters most did.

My Challenge to You . . .

No matter what faith you have or lack, I believe that there is a need to forgive and need to be forgiven in every human spirit. They say that forgiving frees the forgiver.

Take a sheet of paper and write the word *Forgiven* on it. Sit for a time and hold it in your hands. Think about what that means and then accept it. What do you you feel at that moment? If you cannot forgive yourself, then you know what is holding you back from happiness and life itself.

If you are confident enough, place the paper where you and all of your family, perhaps even your co-workers, can see it. Hang it in a window for all the world to see.

Or, even more powerful, send it to someone you have never forgiven and . . .

Set yourself free!

FORGIVE, AND YOU WILL BE FORGIVEN.

Luke 6:37

I wish you enough

gain

to satisfy

your wanting.

gain

What have we gained from life that is of real value?

I hope that when answering that question, you put very few things on your list. I pray that most of the gains in your life have been experiences and knowledge. I hope that what you hold dear and significant is a collection of moments and memories.

For in every experience—good or bad—there is a lesson to be learned. These stories are a reflection of all those wonderful learning moments in life. I hope you gain something from reading them.

My friend...
I wish you enough gain to satisfy your wanting.

"ASK, AND IT WILL BE GIVEN TO YOU; SEEK,
AND YOU WILL FIND; KNOCK, AND IT WILL BE
OPENED TO YOU. FOR EVERYONE WHO ASKS
RECEIVES, AND HE WHO SEEKS FINDS, AND TO
HIM WHO KNOCKS IT WILL BE OPENED."

Matthew 7:7–8

The Man Behind the Moon

Through the years I've spoken with, smiled at, and sung about my forever confidante, making it the focus of many a lonely night.

I've walked the shores of distant lands with its familiar face looking after me. I have cried and laughed a hundred times over love lost and love gained. I have searched along the mountainside, eagerly looking for a better, clearer view of its coming and going.

Seeing it unexpectedly fuller, brighter, and in greater detail, I have rushed to a phone to share it with someone, with anyone who would appreciate the afterglow of day.

Growing up thinking it really was made of cheese, I decided after seeing it through a telescope, it had to be Swiss cheese.

In love songs they call it by name: "Moon River," "Fly Me to the Moon," "Shine On, Harvest Moon," "It's Only a Paper Moon," "Blue Moon," "Moonlight Sonata," and so many more.

But what has always perplexed with me is when they speak about "the man in the moon."

I just could never see him.

Although the moon and I go way back—to this very day, I cannot go out at night without looking for my friend—I will not begin to try to convince you that the moon got me through it all.

No, like everything else in my life, it was the Man behind the moon. The Creator of all things.

When I stood on the shore, His waves danced at my feet, washing away my cares.

When I cried because young love was ripping my heart out, He lifted my spirits by reminding me that love will forever be a part of my life.

When I swooned at the very thought of someone loving me in return, He gently said, "I told you so."

And even when I cursed the night
And wished the moon away,
He always seemed to make things right
By giving me the day.

The sun will shine, the birds will sing,
And I promise very soon—
You'll see the joy that He will bring:
The Man behind the moon.

WHEN I CONSIDER YOUR HEAVENS,
THE WORK OF YOUR FINGERS,
THE MOON AND THE STARS,
WHICH YOU HAVE ORDAINED,
WHAT IS MAN THAT YOU ARE
MINDFUL OF HIM,
AND THE SON OF MAN THAT YOU VISIT HIM?

Psalm 8:3—4

The Waiting Room

This isn't one of my stories about meeting someone—although those stories are my favorite to write.

This isn't a message professing that I've discovered the secret to life and, having read it, you will be changed forever.

It's also not one of those ten-steps-to-anything. I have been urged by my professional peers to create such lists. "People love numbers. They love easy steps to accomplish their dreams," one friend told me.

There are no easy steps to accomplish your dreams. Well, okay, there are two. If you want to have friends, be one. If you want to be loved, love unconditionally.

This message, however, comes from a note I found on top of the dresser in my bedroom.

I write notes all the time. I leave notes everywhere. That's good and bad.

I most likely have come up with some brilliant ideas through the years. Well, perhaps I'm giving myself too much credit using the word *brilliant*. Okay, really good ideas.

But I write them down whenever and wherever it's convenient. Like on napkins in a restaurant, the edge of my newspaper, the back of a sales receipt, and—forgive me—a sheet of toilet paper once. Maybe twice.

I lose them. I throw them away, and, yes, I flush them.

This particular note was buried in a small pile of other notes, receipts, clippings, and so forth that I had "filed" under my cologne and morning meds.

The note simply said, "The waiting room."

Now what could I possibly see in that?

My life. Maybe yours.

I can't remember exactly when I wrote it or where I was, but I can remember the feeling I had when I heard it.

I immediately saw a room full of people. Some were standing, some were sitting, and a few were crouched down in a corner leaning against the wall.

Why were we there? We were all waiting. Not in a doctor's office or as if applying for a job. We were waiting for life. We were waiting for our dreams to come true or for our fears to stop.

No one was speaking, no one was smiling, no one even acknowledged the others. We were just waiting.

That was—and is—the problem. We spend too much time waiting and not enough time moving on, acting upon, attempting to fulfill a dream or calm our fears. If I could see the sign on the door of that room, it would most likely say, "Entitlement."

As if life owes us something. As if God has to do something. As if we deserve something we don't sacrifice for.

My life. Always waiting for the break. Always expecting that the phone will ring or someone will stumble across something I have written and immediately sweep me off my feet with promises of success.

Like the scene from a 1930s musical where the young man is asked to fill in for the lead because he broke his leg.

"Ah, go ahead, Joe. You can do it. I wasn't meant to have this part. This might be your big break," says the injured actor. Sure enough, an agent just happens to be there and bam!—he's a star.

Or the old story of the beautiful girl at the soda fountain who gets the chance of a lifetime.

The waiting room is full of people just waiting for life to come knocking. Why? Not because they worked hard, but because they believe they are entitled to it.

I've been there out of fear too.

I'm the one crouched in the corner, leaning against the wall.

That day I was afraid to go on. Life isn't fair, and if I try again I'll only fail. All I really need to do is pray, and God will make it all go away.

God feeds the smallest bird, but He doesn't throw the food into the nest. That is why He gave them wings.

The waiting room.

Someday my ship will come in.

That's the day I'll be at the airport.

My friend, sometimes you need to swim out to meet the ship. Sometimes you need to go out past the break of the waves into the current to catch a ride.

You won't catch it in the waiting room.

You won't be called on to fill in for the lead if you're not at rehearsals.

You won't be discovered if you're sippin' soda at the corner store. You need to sign up for the audition. You need to show up at their door. You need to knock until your knuckles hurt—and keep knocking until someone answers.

You need to get down on your knees and pray, and you need to stand up for what you believe.

The waiting room is crowded.
You'll not find happiness there.
And life at times is difficult
And often seems unfair.
The truth, my friend, is hard to take,
But in the truth you'll find
That happiness is not a place,
It's just a state of mind.

My friend, it is time to leave the waiting room.

FOR I KNOW THE THOUGHTS THAT I THINK
TOWARD YOU, SAYS THE LORD, THOUGHTS
OF PEACE AND NOT OF EVIL, TO GIVE YOU A
FUTURE AND A HOPE.

Jeremiah 29:11

It's Not Enough

It's not enough to want better things for yourself.

      You must find ways to make things better.

It's not enough to say the world is in turmoil.

      You must find ways to bring peace into it.

It's not enough to point at others and blame them for what is wrong.

      You must welcome them in and ask how you can

        help them make it right.

It's not enough to say, "Someone ought to do something about it!"

      You are someone, so do it!

It's not enough to pray and ask for God's help.

      You must thank him for the challenge and the

        opportunity to learn from it.

It's not enough to tell a child what is right.

      You must be what is right so he can learn from your example.

It's not enough to blame your government for what is wrong.

      You must participate in the process to make it right.

It's not enough to wish.

      You must work to make it so.

It's not enough to ask.

      You must give to earn the right.

It's not enough to say, "I tried!"

> You must try and try again.

It's not enough to want to be loved.

> You must learn how to love first.

It's not enough say, "I care."

> You must show how much and why.

It's not enough to wake up.

> You must thank God you did.

It's not enough to just earn a living.

> You must create a life.

It's not enough to begin.

> You must always follow through.

It's not enough to have a friend.

> You must learn to be one too.

It's not enough to believe in someone.

> You must tell them so.

I believe in you!

BE DOERS OF THE WORD,
AND NOT HEARERS ONLY.

James 1:22

I wish you enough

loss

to appreciate

all that you
possess.

loss

Here I go again. How could I wish someone loss?

Well, if you haven't discovered a pattern here, then you haven't been paying much attention.

"For what profit is it to a man if he gains the whole world, and loses his own soul?" (Matthew 16:26).

As a father, I naturally want only the best for my children. As painful as it may be, significant lessons in their lives will come from pain and loss. Having that balance of joy and pain teaches us how important the little things are and helps us realize that our treasures in life really are bountiful.

So here I share stories of loss and lessons learned.

THROUGH THE LORD'S MERCIES
WE ARE NOT CONSUMED,
BECAUSE HIS COMPASSIONS FAIL NOT.
THEY ARE NEW EVERY MORNING....

Lamentations 3:22—23

I Learned to Live

"You know, I almost died once," he said.

"Really? What happened?" I asked.

"Nothing!" he said. "Except I learned to live."

We create what we want in our lives. I am sure you've heard it all before: "What you think about the most manifests in your life." "You reap what you sow." "If you believe it, you can achieve it."

Of all the principles of success and happiness, that one singular concept is the absolute truth. It is the key to all success in life.

But it can also be the key to failure and even death.

Pete is a friend of mine. One of those people you call "friend," but you really don't know everything about. Just when you think you have him figured out, he tells you something completely surprising. Something even brilliant.

"Did I ever tell you about the time I thought I was going to die?" he asked.

"No, I don't think I've heard that one," I replied.

"In reality, I almost caused my death. You see I went through a period in my life when it seemed everything went wrong physically. It seemed to be one thing after another. Some of the things were identifiable and treated. The doctor knew just what to do, and he did it. But he had 'concerns,' as he put it. It was those concerns that nearly killed me," he said.

Pete is one of those people who is rarely serious. I mean, it's not that he tells jokes all the time, but he's just happy. So hearing and seeing this side of him really caught my attention.

"Bob, I went through a series of tests that started me on a downhill slide. One after another, they revealed more and more possibilities. It was like when you take your car in because you hear a noise, and the mechanic tells you, 'It could be any number of things. It could cost you fifty bucks, or we may need to drop your engine. Then you're talking big bucks.' And what is it that always happens? It costs you big bucks."

"Boy, I can relate to that," I told him.

"Well, because I believe in the worst, I felt the facts were staring me in the face. This was the end of my life," he said.

"What do you think happened to me?" he continued. "My whole world came to a halt. I became depressed. The world looked dark and gloomy. The more I thought that way, the more it became a reality. I was, in fact, creating the world I imagined. I became so physically sick and mentally depressed thinking that I was going to die, that I actually was dying. My body suffered terribly. So much so that I ended up in the hospital, malnourished and depressed."

"So what changed you? What did you do to turn things around?" I asked.

"A young man. A teen who had been in a car accident. He must have had every bone in his body broken. His face was so badly damaged that they operated on him at least a dozen times. When I was in the hospital, I met him. One day he asked what was wrong with me, and I couldn't explain it. I kept saying, 'They aren't sure.'"

"He said, 'Well, that's stupid. How can you fix something that isn't broken? Now me, I had a lot of fixing 'cause everything was broken. The only thing that wasn't broken was my will to live.'"

Pete stopped for a moment and just looked around.

"That's what was broken. My will to live. I had chosen to believe that I was dying, and by doing so I created it. I made it a reality. My will was the one thing that all the doctors in the world couldn't fix. My will was the one thing, the ultimate thing, that only I was in control of. My will was the answer."

"What happened to this young man?" I asked.

"He went on to college, graduated, and now owns his own company. He teaches safety in the workplace to large corporations around the world. And, from what I understand, he tells his story to high school students as a way of giving something back."

"And you, my friend? How did you ever pull out of it?" I asked.

"I willed it to be so. The very next day I stood in front of the mirror in the bathroom and had a good talk with the guy looking back at me. We both agreed that life was too precious to waste. I made up this phrase and hung it everywhere I lived."

He reached in his wallet and handed me a note that read:

> Today I take control of my life. I will permit nothing
> to interfere with my full enjoyment of each and every
> moment that God has granted me. I am deserving of
> all the joy and happiness that this day has to offer.
> There is nothing that God and I can't accomplish. I
> will nourish my body with the best and purest food.
> I will nourish my mind with nothing but the most
> positive thoughts. I will feed my soul with the Word
> of God and know that, when my time on this earth is
> over, I will have lived purely, fully, and faithfully.

So what life have you created? Are you living fully or dying slowly?

Begin to live again. Take control of your life.

"The only thing that wasn't broken was my will to live!" he said.

Learn to live!

THEREFORE HUMBLE YOURSELVES UNDER THE MIGHTY HAND OF GOD, THAT HE MAY EXALT YOU IN DUE TIME, CASTING ALL YOUR CARE UPON HIM, FOR HE CARES FOR YOU.

1 Peter 5:6–7

Even in Death There Is Perfection

I am shaking my head as I sit down to write this. I just can't understand why this happens to me so many times. I am not complaining. I am in awe of the idea that God would permit me to be a part of this precious, sacred moment, time and again.

A bird is dying.

Late yesterday afternoon, as I walked past the feeders, I was startled to find a small sparrow sitting inside the bird feeder cage. I oftentimes stand motionless near the feeder, watching the birds come and go.

I talk to them. I smile. I fill the palm of my hand with seed and gently offer it up to them, hoping to gain their trust.

It doesn't happen.

But I do have my moments. Mostly when one is dying.

This little one had all the signs of approaching death. The feathers were all disheveled, and its tiny feet were curled up underneath. We just stared at each other for a few moments while I offered a soothing word or two.

I slowly reached toward the bird and began stroking the top of its head. Its eyes blinked slowly, almost indicating appreciation for the attention.

I stopped for a moment and noted the rapid breathing had paused, giving the appearance that the bird had passed.

Then suddenly it began breathing again.

I reached inside the cage and gently picked up the bird. This time I stroked the feathers on its back and stomach.

Suddenly it flew from my hand.

"I thought you were dying!" I said.

It landed in the nearby lilac bush, and I went about my day.

My wife, Marianne is out of town today. She called me just before she left to tell me about our dog Ricky.

"I was in a hurry to leave, and I couldn't get him to come back in the house," she said. "I had to go looking for him. I found him standing over a small bird. I thought it was dead, but the poor thing was breathing. I picked it up and placed it near the trellis so that the wandering cats couldn't get to it."

I shared my own experience with her before she hung up.

When I came home, I searched the area where she had left it. I have a special place in the yard where I bury the birds that I have come to know. But the bird was nowhere to be found.

"I bet that cat got to it. I'll just try to convince myself that it got better and flew away," I said.

A little later, I came back from grocery shopping and let the dogs out. Ricky stopped in his tracks, just below the feeders. You got it. The bird was lying there again.

I picked it up and said, "Well, old friend. I guess you missed me."

I walked into the yard and sat in the sunshine holding the bird. I had no idea what I could do with it. I knew I should just place it back where it had been, and let nature do its thing. But what if I were supposed to play a role in this? It's happened so many times before, so I would be a fool to think otherwise.

Once again the little bird suddenly flew from my hand into the bushes. This time it crashed to the ground. I couldn't stand the thought of just leaving it there. You know—the cat. So I climbed over the fence and tried to get it.

The bird took off, and I stood there laughing at my silliness.

No, its life was not over yet.

Just a short time ago, the bird returned to the base of the feeder. Yes, Ricky found it. This time I picked it up and placed it in a nearby birdhouse. I went through all the trouble of getting the screwdriver to open it up and carefully place the bird inside with its head sticking out the opening.

"What a view!" I told him. As sorry as I felt about this, I really just figured the tiny creature would die right there, but in its final moments it would have a perfect view of all it had once loved.

I checked periodically and saw that the small head was still in the same position—eyes wide open and dreaming of better days.

You know what I'm going to tell you, don't you?

Yes, I found the bird back at the base of the feeder. It was still breathing and bright eyed, so I picked it up and gave it the same loving attention I had given it before.

This time I took the lid from one of the plastic bottles I had in the recycling bin. I filled it with water and placed the bird's head slightly above the water. I dipped the beak into the shallow cap and watched it take a few small sips.

Patiently, I tried again and again until I felt it was refreshed.

This time I placed the bird back in the feeder cage where I had originally found it. It stayed there for more than an hour. But I just now looked out the window, and I am sorry to say, I can see it on the ground, struggling to fly off with its friends.

I try desperately to offer stories with happy endings, but I can't always do that. I spoke to God about all of this. I know He could easily renew its strength and make it perfect again. But there is perfection in everything God does.

Even in death.

Yes, I thought about putting it out of its misery. I thought about placing it in a box to protect it. But maybe, just maybe, the plan was for me to do all I could humanly do and trust that God would do the rest.

I am reminded of the song . . .

Let not your heart be troubled,
his tender word I hear,
and resting on his goodness,
I lose my doubts and fears;
though by the path he leadeth
but one step I may see:
His eye is on the sparrow,
and I know he watches me.

Charles Hutchinson Gabriel and Civilla D. Martin

ARE NOT TWO SPARROWS SOLD FOR A COPPER
COIN? AND NOT ONE OF THEM FALLS TO THE
GROUND APART FROM YOUR FATHER'S WILL. . . .
DO NOT FEAR THEREFORE; YOU ARE OF MORE
VALUE THAN MANY SPARROWS.

Matthew 10:29, 31

The Secret to a Long Life

"It's a treasure more valuable than gold," the young girl said. "I wouldn't trade it for anything!"

They had gathered for a family celebration, they said. Oh, not a birthday, anniversary, or birth. They were celebrating death. That's right. A celebration of dying.

I know to some of you it might sound odd. Death is sad and mournful. There is no happiness or joy in losing someone you love, you would say. But for some death is joy filled. It's a crossing over to a better place. It's a spiritual completion and a holy event.

For Amy, this death meant getting the best gift ever.

Amy was very close to her grandmother. They visited often and shared some wonderful moments. When she was very small, they played together, walked together, and shared together. When Amy was sick, Grandma would stay with her so Mom and Dad could go to work. They loved each other in all situations and prayed together about their deepest concerns.

Like the time Amy fell while she was carrying her mom's best vase. Without hesitation Amy turned to Grandma and said, "It's prayer time. This one's a big one, Grandma." I believe that Amy thought that her grandma had as much to do with healing and fixing things as God did. Maybe even more. That's how much Amy trusted her grandma. Their love could withstand anything life threw their way.

But it was inevitable. There would certainly come a day when the realities of time and growing older would gain the upper hand. This time Grandma couldn't kiss it and make it better. Grandma couldn't pray this one away. You see, Grandma was dying. It was her time—but what a splendid time it was.

It was spring, and the flowers that she and Amy attended to each year were in full bloom. You might think that this is the perfect time to be alive. But Grandma convinced Amy otherwise. At ninety-one, she had lived a full life. She had no regrets. Except perhaps leaving Amy alone. But she had taken care of that too.

"Amy," she whispered quietly, "in my closet at home, there is a small wooden box. It has your name on it. In it is all that I can give you. All that I hold dear. In that box is the secret to living a long life."

No, she didn't leave a fortune behind. She had no diamonds or pearls to pass on. What she left was her secret to life. On her final day, she called Amy to her side. They reflected back on a lifetime of love, happiness, and commitment. They laughed and cried and before saying good-bye, Grandma pulled her close and kissed her on the forehead. Then she gently fell into a deep and final sleep. A sleep that would take her home to the grandest celebration of all.

Days after her passing, Amy retrieved the box from Grandma's closet. She took it out to the kitchen table where they had shared so many happy moments together. Placing the old wooden box on the table, she carefully opened it.

There inside Amy found an envelope with the words "The Secret to a Long Life." Her heart raced with the thought that Grandma had gone to all this trouble just for her. She held the note close to her chest and said out loud, "I love you Grandma! Thanks!"

Inside the envelope was one index card. On it were written four words . . . "Live until you die!"

Amy roared with laughter. She ran out of the house and down the street to where her mom was. Together, they read the note and laughed until it hurt.

Somewhere in all the laughter, Amy and her mom decided to hold a special celebration every year. The big day was the day Grandma died. Everyone who knew and loved Grandma would come home for the big event, no matter where life had taken them.

There is a profound truth in those simple words, for I have found many who died long ago in spirit and hope, yet they continued to breathe.

For Amy and her family, it's not a secret anymore. It's a celebration of . . .

Learning to live.

I HAVE FOUGHT THE GOOD FIGHT, I HAVE FINISHED THE RACE, I HAVE KEPT THE FAITH.

2 Timothy 4:7

SEVEN

I wish you enough

"Hellos"

to get you through
the final

"Good-bye."

hellos

"Hello, again hello!"

I sing that song for my father. It is another one of my Neil Diamond favorites. I can remember how important it was to hear my father's voice on the other end of the phone.

Through the years, as my two sons decided to grow up, I have wrapped those words around hearing their voices too.

There's an excitement about the word *hello*. I think about holidays and all types of reunions. When calling someone, hearing them say "Hello" makes me sigh. It says, "Oh good. You are there. I want you to be. I need to speak with you."

I would give anything to hear my parents say it one more time . . . "Hello!"

It is the opposite I dread so much.

My friend...
I wish you enough hellos
to get you through the final good-bye.

NOW MAY THE GOD OF HOPE FILL YOU WITH
ALL JOY AND PEACE IN BELIEVING, THAT YOU
MAY ABOUND IN HOPE BY THE POWER OF
THE HOLY SPIRIT.

Romans 15:13

So, How Is Your Life?

He was a most remarkable man. A man of years, each one clearly mapped out upon his face.

Clean, well kept, but not pretentious in his style or dress. I shook his hand and felt a mix of gentle wear and hardened, calloused, leatherlike skin. I would guess that he had labored most of his life, perhaps forced to stop now long enough to heal somewhat.

His movie star blue eyes held me momentarily transfixed as they seemed to cut into my heart. He wouldn't have noticed me staring at him, for he is legally blind. But he would sense the hesitation in my voice if I didn't respond immediately to his first question: "So, how is your life?"

That question alone was enough to halt me in my tracks. It bears repeating.

"You asked, 'How is my life?'"

"Yes," he said.

"I would be better prepared to answer how is my day," I suggested.

"That's too easy," he said. "I think we need to keep tabs on our life as a whole."

I thought for a moment and simply asked, "Why?"

"We tend to nitpick. We can so easily take one day and dissect it. It is easy to say you are having a bad day. Or simply write it off as 'one of those days.' But when we broaden the view, we take much more into consideration. Life in general will at least be 'good,' 'okay,' or 'it could be better,'" he explained.

"So, you cut right to the chase and ask for an overall rating," I said.

"If I can get a few folks each day to see the big picture and realize there is more good in their life than one bad day, I might even change their outlook on this very day," he said.

"So, how is your life?" I asked of him.

"Wonderful so far. Thanks for asking."

Then he said one more thing that stayed with me: "I'm on the shady side of sunset."

How powerful! It seems to me that we often see life as beginnings and endings. Sunrises depict a new dawn, an exciting adventure ahead. Sunsets make us think of endings. Like "riding off into the sunset."

This man knew his life, his time on this earth, was coming to a close.

"I do hope the sun sets slowly for you. You have so many more people to ask the big question," I told him.

And before I left, I promised him I'd help. Let me begin by asking you:

"So, how is your life?"

NOW MAY THE GOD OF HOPE FILL YOU WITH ALL JOY AND PEACE IN BELIEVING, THAT YOU MAY ABOUND IN HOPE BY THE POWER OF THE HOLY SPIRIT.

Romans 15:13

The Last Steps

It was a very hot and humid day. People who work outside for a living should just go home when it's like this. But if they did, the world would stop spinning, I suppose.

The world was not going to stop for this man, though. I met him as he was putting the finishing touches on the front steps of a newly built home.

"I can't believe you are working in this heat," I said.

"I've worked in the heat, the cold, all kinds of weather. I even worked in the middle of a hurricane once," the man replied with a grin.

He was a slender man. I'm surprised the hurricane didn't blow him away. His hands and face bore witness to what appeared to be decades of labor in the sun. I believe you could light a match on the back of his dried-out hands.

"How long have you done this?" I asked.

"Since I was old enough to pick up a hammer," he said proudly. "But today . . . today, these are my last steps."

"Is there something wrong? You look like there's a few more miles left on you," I said.

"It's time for me to stop. Sometimes you just have to tell yourself, 'Stop already!' That's what I did this morning. My wife got up early—just as she has for nearly forty years—to make me breakfast, hot coffee, and a little inspiration. I looked in the mirror and said, 'That's it.' She said, 'Are you sure?' And I said, 'Sure enough!'"

"You said she makes you a little inspiration. How does she do that?"

"She takes the Bible and flops it on the table in front of me. Wherever it opens, she runs her finger down the page and where she stops, she reads. It's never failed to mean something special that day."

"What did she read today that made you say, 'That's it'?

"Genesis 2:2: 'and on the seventh day God ended His work which He had done, and He rested on the seventh day from all His work which He had done'."

"And why was that significant to you?" I asked.

"I've been working nearly every day of my life. Sundays included. My wife put up with it, but oftentimes she went to church on her own. Today being Sunday, she didn't flop the book down, she nearly threw it at me. It fell open to that page almost by accident."

"Why do you say 'almost by accident'?"

He started laughing and shaking his head and said, "She had it paper clipped and underlined. I saw it as a sign. Not from God." He laughed so hard, he could hardly speak. "A sign from my wife!"

"So this is the last job?"

"Well, you can take the carpenter off the job, but you can't make him put down his hammer," he said, still chuckling. "But, ultimately, these are the last steps."

"You must be proud of what you have accomplished in your life."

"You know, most people have no idea what I do. They see me working as a carpenter. But I create place. By that I mean that I create something from nothing, and you call it home. Like these steps I'm finishing. They will lead this family into a safe place where dreams and love come alive. I've seen newlyweds cross over my thresholds to begin a new life together. But I've also seen people carried out at the end of their lives, going out the door one final time," he said as he looked up at the new door on this home.

"In the places I've created, celebrations were held. Servicemen came home to them, college kids left them and returned as graduates. Christmas trees were erected in them; and people of all faiths prayed in them. Laughter and tears were shared in these same places. I created them. Now it's time to stop."

He grabbed his hammer and, with one final nail, ended a lifetime of creation and commitment. Then he headed off to his own place in time, making . . .

The last steps.

WELL DONE, GOOD AND FAITHFUL SERVANT . . . ENTER INTO THE JOY OF YOUR LORD.

Matthew 25:21

A Change of Heart

It's the world we live in that made me feel this way. Otherwise, I wouldn't have thought for a moment about sitting next to that beautiful young girl.

My recent trip to Kentucky ran smoothly except for a near two-hour delay in Pittsburgh. I must admit I have never had a major problem while flying across this great country. In fact, I believe this was the first time I had ever experienced a delay that long.

But I always tell my travel agent that if ever I need to be delayed, let it be in Pittsburgh. They have the greatest restaurants and enough shops to keep me busy for hours.

They finally announced boarding. Now I don't believe for a moment that I'm the only person who goes through this. From the moment I enter the plane, I start scanning ahead to see my seat. *Who's sitting next to me on this flight?* I wonder. *Is there anyone in my seat already?* That's happened a few times. And of course, I always look to see if there are any screaming babies nearby.

Flight time is precious time for me. I sleep, write, or read. So screaming babies and frequent-bathroom people can become a problem.

Today my seat is next to a beautiful young girl who appears to be about twelve years old. As I approach my seat, she seems nervous, perhaps a little apprehensive, and, I must say, very disappointed. You see, walking in front of me was this handsome, male teenager. I could see that sparkle in her eye dim as he walked by and I sat down. I'll admit I was nervous and concerned. She was traveling alone, and I was one of those strangers her parents probably told her not to talk to.

"Hi! My name is Bob," I said.

"Hello!" she replied, without giving her name.

Then we spent the next one hour and fifteen minutes not saying a word.

She was a typical kid. She never sat still for longer than five minutes. Every few minutes she reached into her carry-on and pulled out what appeared to be six brushes, four packs of gum and all the empty wrappers, a bag filled with jawbreakers, a tube of rainbow-colored sugar crystals, and a three-foot long piece of licorice. Oh yes, she also ate two bags of airplane peanuts. I gave her mine.

It wasn't until the last fifteen minutes of the flight that I heard it. That sweet-sounding Voice saying, *Give her one of your books!*

"She's only twelve," I argued. She won't find my book interesting. *Do they even know how to read at twelve?* I thought sarcastically.

But again and again I heard the Voice repeat, Give her one of your books! And so I opened one up, signed it, and said, "I am a professional speaker and author. I'd like to give you one of my books, if you would permit me."

She giggled a bit and said, "Yes," followed by, "Thanks!"

I then began to explain the story.

"It's a fictional story based on actual events. I changed the names, but basically much of this is true. My oldest son, Keith, had cancer, and that's part of this book."

"Oh, I'm sorry," she said.

"No need to be. He's doing just fine, thank you. Where are you from?" I asked.

Then for the next ten minutes this young lady never stopped talking. In fact, as we were leaving the plane, she talked and walked backward down the aisle.

Much of what she said was all a blur for me after she said these words: "Wow, I just saw the Hershey Medical Center mentioned in there. Is that where your son went for his cancer treatments?" she asked.

I nodded. "Yes."

"That's where I had my heart transplant," she said with a big bright smile.

Heart transplant. This child had had a heart transplant. Then I took notice. Right at the top of her pink T-shirt, just below her collarbone, the beginnings of a scar peeked out. This vibrant, young, beautiful girl had the heart of a donor. Obviously a young donor whose family cared enough to save another child's life.

She continued to share the details of her stay at Hershey. I continued to listen in amazement, for the story she told was a familiar one. She was the girl down the hall we all had prayed for. I hadn't known how things turned out for her until today.

They say some lives cross because they were meant to. This was more than a chance meeting. I discovered that this child leaving Pittsburgh to go home to Kentucky was a patient in the same hospital, on the same floor of miracles, at the same time my son was there. That little Voice inside of me had kept telling me to give her a copy of my book. I had argued. The Voice won . . . as always.

The last words she said to me were . . . "My mom always told me that God was going to call me home, but then He had a change of heart! Do you get it?" Then she giggled and laughed as she walked through the last door and into the arms of her loving family.

I got it.
I heard the Voice say, "Now you know why!"

PEACE I LEAVE WITH YOU, MY PEACE I GIVE
TO YOU; NOT AS THE WORLD GIVES DO I GIVE
TO YOU. LET NOT YOUR HEART BE TROUBLED,
NEITHER LET IT BE AFRAID.

John 14:27

The Orchid Girl

I could have ordered earlier, but then I would have missed meeting her. She was beautiful and wonderfully intelligent.

You see, God had a plan. There was a lesson here for me in the Peking Chef Restaurant take-out area. And, for once in my life, I was speechless.

Normally, I would have called ahead to place my order. I don't like to sit in restaurants waiting for take-out, but I really needed to get out of the house for a while. I have been working on another book, and I had fried my brain hours earlier. Even this would be a refreshing change in my day.

In the lobby area of this restaurant are four or five potted orchids. I've seen orchids a hundred times, but lately they have grabbed my attention and stolen my heart. We saw some at the garden center just this weekend. I wanted desperately to buy one, but I tend to kill delicate plants like these. My wife urged me to buy one anyway. I declined. "I am destined to love them from afar," I told her.

But then I met Samantha.

"Call me Sam," she insisted.

I was admiring the flowers up close when Sam came running in. Her parents were seated in the restaurant waiting for their meal. Like any other ten-year-old, Sam didn't want to stay seated very long. She insisted on visiting her flower.

"They are beautiful, aren't they?" she said as she entered.

"Incredible! They look so delicate and fragile," I replied.

"They're not, really," she said. "They are actually a tough flower. Everyone thinks they are hard to grow. We have dozens of orchids at home. It just takes a lot of love."

"Anything of value does take a lot of love," I said.

"That's why they mean love, beauty, and wisdom. In China, the orchid represents the innocence of children. A pink orchid is affection. The cattleya orchid means charm and is a favorite for Mother's Day," she said.

"Wow! How is it that you know so much about orchids?" I asked.

"I'm the Orchid Girl," she replied. "My mom told me that I was born from an orchid."

"Really?"

She then turned her head, exposing her left cheek to me. There, on the side of her face just under her long dark hair, was a scar about two inches wide and three inches tall. Not just a straight cut. Clearly the delicate remains of what must have been a very bad accident.

"See, it looks just like an orchid," she said proudly.

And, in truth, it did.

"You must love being the orchid girl," I said.

"Mostly. Sometimes the kids in school laugh at me and call me 'the girl with the orchid face.' I don't like that. But Mom told me that when she was bringing me home from the hospital after I was born, we were in an accident. She thought we would both die. So she prayed to God to give her a sign that everything was going to be all right. She had left her room to visit me down the hall. When she returned, there was an orchid on her pillow. She thinks God placed it there. As I grew up, the scars on my face from the accident turned into the same flower that Mom got from God. So I'm the Orchid Girl."

"Sam, you are one of a kind and very special to God," I said.

"Well, actually there are twenty-five thousand different kinds of orchids. Well, 25,001. There's me. That's how I know orchids are tough, and they mean love. I am loved, and I love everyone back. And I didn't die!" she said with a big, broad smile.

"Mr. Perks?" the cashier called out. "Your takeout is ready."

"What an honor it has been for me to meet you" I said.

"Thanks" she replied quietly.

"I have admired that flower every time I came in here, but I never realized how beautiful it really was until I met you," I told her.

"I'll tell God. Maybe He will give you one too!" she said as she ran back to her table.

I headed home listening to our local classical radio station. I couldn't get the image of that beautiful child out of my mind. Or that delicate orchid scar on her cheek.

I thought about how wonderful it was that her mom had turned that scar into something beautiful for her. Growing up with a scar like that could cause a child to lose her self-esteem. But I believe Sam's scar, over time, looked more like a beauty mark.

I couldn't wait for my wife to come from work. *She won't believe this one*, I thought. *Or will she?*

As I came around the corner, I saw that my wife had just pulled into the driveway. Anxiously, I ran to her as she was taking her bag from the backseat.

"Honey, you won't believe this story! I just met the most incredible . . ." Standing there with an orchid plant in hand, she interrupted me and said: "I know you thought you'd kill it. But on my way home I was driving past the exit of the garden center and, before I knew it, I was inside. The man at the garden center said that they are really easy to take care of. You just need to give it . . ."

"I know. A lot of love," I said. The Orchid Girl told me. You've just answered her prayer."

Beauty isn't always delicate.
Love doesn't always hurt.

I CAN DO ALL THINGS THROUGH CHRIST
WHO STRENGTHENS ME.

Philippians 4:13

Daisy Scent

I look for signs and wonders in everyday life to confirm that I'm on the right path. God sends me people to tell me, show me, or guide me along the way. That's why I write stories. My stories are about those people.

Except this one. This one is about my dog Daisy.

We had Daisy in our lives for over a dozen years. Every second of every day of those wonderful years was a precious gift to us. But as Daisy began to approach about fifteen years of age, her body began to give way.

I can relate to that sometimes.

Daisy began having some serious setbacks. Her arthritis was worsening, although she managed to get around quite nicely . . . considering. We kept her on her daily medication, and her doctor felt she was doing just fine.

Then one day I began to see signs of her failing health. I called the vet. They told me what to watch for, but they explained that ultimately the decision to put Daisy to sleep was all mine. Marianne and I had a conversation about this.

"Hon, do you want me to tell you when the day has come for Daisy, so you can say your good-byes?" I asked.

"Honey, I have said good-bye to her a thousand times already. I know what lies ahead," she told me.

"So you don't want me to tell you?" I asked.

"No."

I prayed for days for one of those magnificent signs from God letting me know when Daisy needed to go home.

I waited. Nothing.

That is, until one night when I wasn't expecting it.

Through the years, every time Marianne and I went away for a few days, we took Daisy to this incredible farm where she was loved and cared for while we were gone. The first time we took her, the owner told me that to make Daisy more comfortable while we were gone, one of us should wear an old T-shirt for a few days and bring it in with her. The scent left on the clothing would keep her comfortable and keep us not too far from her memory.

Now, Daisy slept on a dog mattress next to our bed every night. The mattress was on Marianne's side, so Daisy always slept there.

But this night, it was the oddest thing. Just as we climbed into bed, Daisy came over to my side and lay down on the floor. She had never done that before. She was panting a little, so I petted her for a while, expecting that she would go to her bed as soon as I stopped.

She didn't. She stayed there all night, never moving even when I got up a few times. I would return, and there she was sleeping.

The reason I find this all so fascinating is this: She slept on my T-shirt that I always have lying on the floor. She had curled up on it and made a bed out of it.

The next morning she woke up and could not walk. I had to carry her downstairs. She even had difficulty standing up to eat.

Marianne left for work, and I waited with Daisy.

At 10 a.m., I called the vet and could barely speak. The assistant waited patiently for me to say something. She knew why I was calling.

"Bring her in at 2 p.m.," she said.

I cried so hard when I hung up that I could hardly stand. I held Daisy in my arms, and we sat there.

Some of you may not like this part. Most will understand.

Daisy and I had a party that day. She always loved the crust from the pizza we ate. So that day I ordered a pizza and bought a McDonald's Quarter Pounder with Cheese, no condiments, and we sat on the floor together. I opened the pizza box and let her eat what she wanted. She then ate the burger, and I followed it up with a small dish of vanilla ice cream.

She loved it. So did I.

I didn't call Marianne and tell her about Daisy. Instead, I placed Daisy's picture on the kitchen table, and I bought flowers for her. Yes, they were daisies.

That night we held each other and cried. And, yes, we held that old T-shirt that Daisy had left to comfort us and to keep her not too far from our memories.

It was Daisy "scent."

BLESSED BE THE GOD AND FATHER OF OUR LORD JESUS CHRIST, THE FATHER OF MERCIES AND GOD OF ALL COMFORT, WHO COMFORTS US IN ALL OUR TRIBULATION.

2 Corinthians 1:3–4

good-bye

I hate good-byes!

It's that simple. I'll admit to you right here that even typing the word *good-bye* sets my heart pounding.

Yet, like all negative things, the unavoidable good-bye has value in it.

I know you must have heard this a million times, but realizing that life is unpredictable, that death is inevitable, we learn to value each moment we have.

But the final good-bye still comes as a shock, even though we all accept that our time here on earth cannot last forever.

So love each other as if today were the last day, so that you hold no regrets over never having the chance to say . . . good-bye.

Until then my friends, please know that I love you all!

I Wish You Enough!
Bob Perks

LET NOT YOUR HEART BE TROUBLED; YOU
BELIEVE IN GOD, BELIEVE ALSO IN ME. IN MY
FATHER'S HOUSE ARE MANY MANSIONS; IF IT
WERE NOT SO, I WOULD HAVE TOLD YOU. I GO
TO PREPARE A PLACE FOR YOU. AND IF I GO
AND PREPARE A PLACE FOR YOU, I WILL COME
AGAIN AND RECEIVE YOU TO MYSELF; THAT
WHERE I AM, THERE YOU MAY BE ALSO.

John 14:1–3

ABOUT BOB

*"Reading Bob's stories inspires you.
Hearing him tell his stories changes your life...forever!"*

Bob Perks is president of Creative Motivation and has been speaking and writing for more than twenty years, touching the lives of millions of people. He is a featured columnist with international recognition on Beliefnet.com.

His over twenty years in the non-profit sector has provided first hand knowledge of "Volunteers don't grow on trees . . . nurture the ones you have," a program presented to hundreds of non-profits nationwide.

An inspirational speaker and corporate trainer, he has addressed meetings, conferences, and civic organizations across the U. S., providing training and talks of motivation, people skills, change, stress management, the gender difference, creativity, and listening skills, as applied to business and personal development.

YOU CAN REACH BOB FOR SPEAKING ENGAGEMENTS
BY VISITING HIS WEB SITE: *www.BobPerks.com.*

A FULL COLLECTION OF INSPIRATIONAL GIFTS BASED ON
HIS WRITING IS AVAILABLE AT *www.IWishYouEnough.com.*

His smile is matched only by his heart!
He loves people and it shows!